Magic
MOTIVES

A Method For Developing Jazz Vocabulary

by Dan Haerle

Published by
JAMEY AEBERSOLD JAZZ®
P.O. Box 1244
New Albany, IN 47151-1244
www.jazzbooks.com
ISBN 978-1-56224-291-6

Cover Design by JASON A. LINDSEY

About the Author

Dan Haerle is a composer, performer, educator and ambassador of jazz piano. He is a regents professor emeritus of Jazz Studies at the University of North Texas, where he taught for 34 years. Dan is an active jazz clinician nationally and internationally and has written instructional material used by thousands of musicians worldwide. At the 2012 Jazz Education Network (JEN) conference in Louisville, he was recognized, along with Jamey Aebersold, David Baker and Jerry Coker, in the inaugural class of the LeJENds of Jazz award. Dan was elected a member of the International Association of Jazz Education Hall of Fame in 2003. His participation in a variety of educational programs has benefited countless musicians of all levels of experience. Dan has performed with Clark Terry, Pat Metheny, David Liebman, Freddie Hubbard and numerous other modern jazz leaders. He has recorded multiple albums, featuring his own music as well as jazz standards, with his trio and quartet. He continues to teach jazz piano and improvisation online and at the Dallas School of Music. He is available for residencies and concerts with his trio or quartet.

Contact Dan at http://www.danhaerle.com.

Introduction

The building blocks of all types of music are short fragments, or motives. These motives may be expanded into phrases that express a complete musical idea. In jazz, we call these motives "licks" or "clichés." Sometimes the word "cliché" has a negative connotation, as in "His playing is cliché-ridden!" And, if jazz improvisation is only a series of clichés, this is definitely not good! But all music has its clichés and they are how we recognize jazz, classical, soul, pop and country. In jazz, all artists have their own clichés that make it possible to recognize them individually.

When building a jazz vocabulary, a musician needs a lot of jazz "words." These are motives that are interesting melodically and clearly describe a particular sound or color, such as major, minor, dominant 7th, half-diminished or diminished. These jazz words may be based on arpeggios of a chord or some type of scale motion through the chord. Though it is useful to know the full six-, seven- or eight-note scale that relates to the chord, it is not necessary to use all of the notes to construct motives.

After many years of listening to and playing jazz, I realized that many clichés we all agree sound good come from five-note scales. When these motives are superimposed in the right place on a chord, they zero in on the important part of the sound. This book shows how motives may be developed using only five-note major, minor and diminished scales and how to apply chromatic embellishment to those scales. The "magic" appears when you discover that any motives created from these scales may be superimposed onto a variety of chords with equally good results! When you create a motive based on a five-note minor scale, it may be used 10 different ways. When you use a five-note major scale to create a motive, it may be used 14 different ways!

The various sections of this book discuss and suggest a variety of motives and how to create them. The expansion of motives beyond their five-note range is also dicussed as well as chromatic embellishment. A summary of the applications, or superimpositions, of the motives by chord family and scale type is included.

This book is not the answer to everything concerning jazz improvisation. But, it will help you develop a larger vocabulary of jazz "licks" idiomatic to the music and extremely versatile in their application to chords.

Dan Haerle
Denton, Texas
September 2013

Foreword

I would like to congratulate my friend, Dan Haerle, on his book of improvisation. This is a different approach. Dan has fragmented the scale down to fewer notes so one can create choice motives. I have used this idea all my life. This is a very logical way, in book form, to help all people interested in improving their skills at improvisation ~ Jack Petersen

Thanks

Special thanks to my wife Jill for her patience and understanding while I was focused on this project. Also, she wielded her expertise as an editor in making the book readable and understandable. Thanks, also, to all of my colleagues and musical friends with whom I have had many great moments making music. Finally, thanks to all of my students, past and present. You are a constant inspiration and a source of new ideas for me ~ Dan Haerle

Other books by Dan Haerle

Jazz Piano Voicing Skills – Jamey Aebersold Jazz

Jazz Improvisation, A Pocket Guide – Jamey Aebersold Jazz

Fusion, Volume 109, Playalong – Jamey Aebersold Jazz

Albums by Dan Haerle

Live at Luminous Sound, 2012 – Dan Haerle, piano; Brad Leali, saxophone; James Driscoll, bass; Ed Soph, drums (Available at CDBaby, Amazon, iTunes, etc.)

Aspiration, 2011 – Dan Haerle, piano; Bob Bowman, bass; Jack Mouse, drums (Available at CDBaby, Amazon, iTunes, etc.)

Standard Procedure, 2004 – Dan Haerle, piano; Bob Bowman, bass; Jack Mouse, drums (Available at CDBaby, Amazon, iTunes, etc.)

The Truth of the Matter, 1999 – Dan Haerle, keyboards; Bob Bowman, bass; Jack Mouse, drums (Available at CDBaby, Amazon, iTunes, etc.)

Contents

MORE *JAZZ* BOOKS FROM *JAMEY AEBERSOLD*

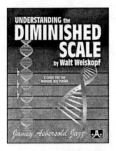

UNDERSTANDING THE DIMINISHED SCALE
by WALT WEISKOPF   CODE: UDS

This long awaited 104 page book is THE defining treatise on the diminished scale. It explains everything you need to know about this versatile scale and how/where to use it in your solos. Includes 12 exercises, 6 common patterns, and 4 classic diminished licks over ii/V7/I tracks aligned to Jamey's popular Vol. 3 play-a-long (sold separately). Also included are 12 etudes, many based on standards, that demonstrate how and where to place diminished scale ideas in the changes.

TARGET AND APPROACH TONES
by JOE RIPOSO   CODE: TAT

Learn the secret to playing long, flowing musical lines that move from one chord change to the other in a smooth, seamless manner. This book explains "approach tones" (a tone or series of tones leading to a chord tone of the next chord - usually by a whole or half step) and "target tones" (tones that resolve your phrases and outline harmony). All great jazz players use this technique to create forward motion, tension/release, and play musical solos that sound "right."

INTERMEDIATE JAZZ IMPROVISATION
by GEORGE BOUCHARD   CODE: IJI

A Study Guide for Developing Soloists. Bridge the gap between playing scales, chords and licks to playing realistic, flowing jazz lines! Specifically designed to build upon the knowledge you already have (basic chord and scale knowledge) to improve your understanding and skills as a soloist. The 2 Play-A-Long CD's include selected tracks from Aebersold Play-A-Longs coordinated with exercises and solo examples played on a separate channel and notated in the book. All parts in the book are transposed for all instruments.

PRACTICING JAZZ
by DAVID BAKER   CODE: BAK

A much heralded jazz practice method from leading educator/performer David Baker. David condenses a wealth of experience and knowledge into practice-specific ideas and exercises for all musicians. Subjects covered include practice goals, techniques and strategies, hearing, transcribing, playing with play-a-longs and "actual" recordings, tune memorization, self evaluation and much more.

THE JAZZ REPERTOIRE
by JERRY COKER   CODE: TJR

by Jerry Coker. Now Available!. Jerry presents an easy-to-understand no nonsense approach for quickly analyzing any tune to make it easier to understand, transpose, and improvise over. Thinking in Roman numerals, recognizing the common elements from which nearly all tunes are derived, and knowing the traditional "road maps" will make you a more prepared and, therefore, a more confident improvisor.

Available from your favorite music source, or visit www.jazzbooks.com for more information.

Magic Motives
Part 1
Five-Note Minor Scales

1. Applications

Here is a five-note D minor scale shown with chord symbols indicating all of its applications. Note its structure: whole-step, half-step, whole-step, whole-step.

Notice where each five-note scale is located in relation to the chord. It's built on the root or 5th of a minor chord, the 5th of a dominant 7th chord, the b9 of an altered dominant chord, the 5th or 9th of a dominant 7th sus4 chord, the 3rd or 7th of a half-diminished chord, and the 3rd or 6th of a major 7th chord. The next example shows the five-note minor scales transposed to apply to C chords of various types. The chord tone on which the scale is built is shown under the first note.

Be sure to play each application of the five-note scales. Play the chord on a keyboard and, if you're not a pianist, hold the sustain pedal down and play the related five-note scale over it on your instrument. I think you will agree that the scale sounds equally good in all locations.

From the previous example, it should be obvious that it will be very helpful if you are comfortable playing five-note minor scales in all keys! This should be part of your daily practice.

The five-note minor scale in all 12 keys:

2. Motive Development

To develop motives, experiment with different types of motion through either the five-note scale or the minor triad it outlines. The examples below begin very simply and gradually become more complex. Start with motives that use only the five notes in the scale. Chromatic embellishment of motives will be discussed later. The scale numbers are written under the notes.

Motives built from a five-note D minor scale:

3. Motive Expansion

Motives do not have to be confined within the five-note range of the scale. In fact, a very well-known motive, the "Cry Me a River" lick, comes from a five-note minor scale. In the first example below, you will see the original motive and its expansion with the first two notes up an octave. Also shown are a couple of other variations on expanding the motive.

4. Chromatic Embellishment

In addition to the five notes in the scale, there are five chromatic notes inside and around the scale. All of these notes are available for embellishing and adding chromatic interest to motives. Potentiall you could use 10 of the 12 notes in a motive, but don't destroy the clarity of the minor scale! As much as we like it, chromaticism destroys tonality if the emphasis isn't on the non-chromatic notes.

A five-note minor scale and its embellishing tones:

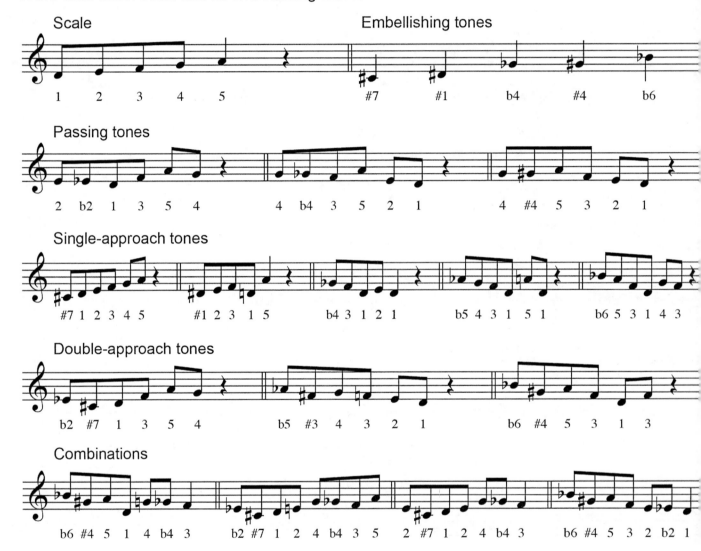

5. Motives Applied to Chord Progressions

The first phrase uses the same five-note D minor scale for both the II chord (built on the root) and the V chord (built on the 5th).

This phrase uses a five-note A minor scale for the II chord (built on the 5th) and a five-note Ab minor scale for the V chord (built on the b9th). This allows for a descending chromatic motion.

The next phrase uses a five-note F minor scale for the II chord (built on the 3rd) and a five-note Ab minor scale for the V chord (built on the b9th). This creates an ascending motion of a 3rd.

This phrase uses a five-note F minor scale for the II chord and a five-note Ab minor scale for the V chord, as in the previous example. This time the 2-1-5-3-2-1 motives have been expanded to create the "Cry Me a River" lick.

The next phrase is a III-VI-II-V-I (turnaround) progression. It uses minor scales built on the 5th of the minor chords and minor scales built on the b9 of the altered dominant chords. There are opportunities for a large variety of chromatic sequences. Notice that the same 5-3-2-1 motive is used on both of the dominant chords.

This is another turnaround progression with a different motive used on each chord.

6. Practice Patterns for Motive Embellishment

Here are a couple of practice patterns using all of the notes of a five-note D minor scale and all five embellishing tones. Though they are extremely chromatic, the D minor sound is still clear. Learning these in all keys will increase your security with both the scales and the chromatic embellishment of them.

Magic Motives
Part 2
Five-Note Major Scales

1. Applications

Here is a five-note C major scale shown with chord symbols indicating all of its applications.
Note its structure: whole-step, whole-step, half-step, whole-step.

Notice where each five-note scale is located in relation to the chord. It is built on the root, or 9th, of a major 7th or dominant 7th chord; the 3rd of a minor 7th chord, or major 7th #5 chord; the 4th of a dominant 7th sus4, or minor 7th chord; the 5th of a major 7th, or minor #7 chord; the #5 of an altered dominant 7th; the 6th of a half-diminished chord; and the 7th of a minor 7th, or half-diminished 7th.

The next example shows the five-note major scales transposed to apply to C chords of various types. The chord tone on which the scale is built is shown under the first note.

Be sure to play each application of the five-note scales. Play the chord on a keyboard and, if you're not a pianist, hold the sustain pedal down and play the related five-note scale over it on your instrument. I think you will agree that the scale sounds equally good in all locations.

From the previous example, it should be obvious that it will be very helpful if you are comfortable playing five-note major scales in all keys. This should be part of your daily practice.

The five-note major scale in all 12 keys:

2. Motive Development

To develop motives, experiment with different types of motion through either the five-note scale or the major triad it outlines. Below, you will see some examples that begin very simply and gradually become more complex. Begin with motives that use only the five notes in the scale. Chromatic embellishment of motives will be discussed later. Motives from a five-note C major scale:

3. Motive Expansion

otives do not have to be confined to the five-note range of the scale. Any notes in the motive
ay be moved up or down an octave to create larger intervals. Here are some five-note major
:ale motives with their expansions. The scale numbers are written under the notes.

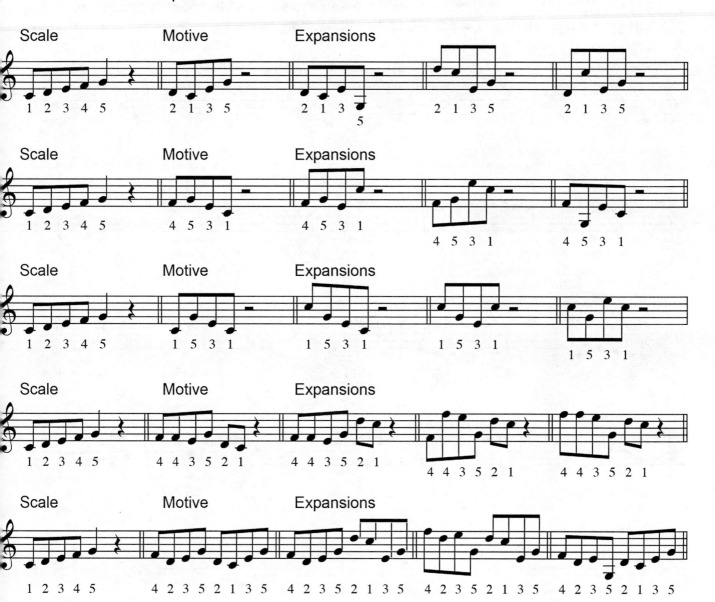

4. Chromatic Embellishment

In addition to the five notes in the scale, there are five chromatic notes inside and around the scale. All of these notes are available for embellishing and adding chromatic interest to motives. Potentially you could use 10 of the 12 notes in a motive, but don't destroy the clarity of the major scale! As much as we like it, chromaticism destroys tonality if the emphasis isn't on the non-chromatic notes. The next example shows a five-note major scale and its embellishing tones.

5. Motives Applied to Chord Progressions

The first phrase uses a five-note C major scale for the II chord (built on the 7th), and the same five-note G major scale for both the V chord (built on the root) and the I chord (built on the 5th).

This phrase uses a five-note G major scale for all three chords of the II-V-I progression.

The next phrase uses a five-note C major scale for the II chord (built on the 7th), a five-note A major scale for the V chord (built on the 9th) and a five-note G major scale for the I chord (built on the 5th).

This phrase uses a five-note C major scale for the II chord, a five-note Eb major scale for the V chord and a five-note D major scale for the I chord.

The next phrase is a III-VI-II-V-I (turnaround) progression. It uses five-note major scales built on the #5th of the altered dominant chords and a five-note major scale built on the 5th of the I chord.

This is another turnaround progression, using the same scales as the previous example, with the same motive used on each chord.

6. Practice Patterns for Motive Embellishment

Here are a couple of practice patterns that use all of the notes of a five-note C major scale and all five embellishing tones. Though they are extremely chromatic, the C major sound is still clear. Learning these in all keys will increase security with both the scales and the chromatic embellishment of them.

Magic Motives
Part 3
Five-Note Diminished Scales

1. Applications

There are only three transpositions of the eight-note diminished scale. Each one of those relates to four different chords (keys). There are four different five-note scales that may be derived from each of the scales. Note its structure: whole-step, half-step, whole-step, half-step.

In the first example, notice that each group of four five-note diminished scales comes from the same eight-note diminished scale.

Each one of these five-note scales may be superimposed on the root, 3rd, 5th or 7th of a diminished 7th chord as seen above. These scales may also be superimposed on the 3rd, 5th, 7th or b9th of a dominant 7b9 chord. The example below shows those applications.

Be sure to play each application of the five-note scales. Play the chord on a keyboard and, if you're not a pianist, hold the sustain pedal down and play the related five-note scale over it on your instrument. I think you will agree that the scale sounds equally good in all locations.

13

2. Motive Development

To develop motives, experiment with different types of motion through either the five-note scale or the diminished triad it outlines. The examples below begin very simply and gradually become more complex. Start with motives that use only the five notes in the scale. Chromatic embellishment of motives will be discussed later.

Motives from a five-note C diminished scale:

3. Motive Expansion

Motives don't have to be confined within the five-note range of the scale. Any notes in the motive ma be moved up or down an octave to create larger intervals. Here are some diminished five-note scale motives with their expansions. The scale numbers are written under the notes.

14

4. Chromatic Embellishment

In addition to the five notes in the scale, there are four chromatic notes inside and around the scale. All of these notes are available for embellishing and adding chromatic interest to motives. Potentially, you could use nine of the 12 notes in a motive, but don't destroy the clarity of the diminished scale! As much as we like it, chromaticism destroys tonality if the emphasis isn't on the non-chromatic notes. The next example shows a five-note diminished scale and its embellishing tones.

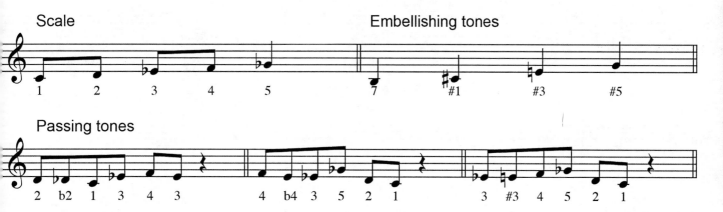

Magic Motives
Part 4
Applications to Tunes

Working with five-note scales will help develop vocabulary (licks) that can be used over all chord types. But, if motives are played in a fragmented manner, there won't be an interesting flow through the chord progression from measure to measure. This part of the book will show how to connect the motives over the chord progressions in tunes.

Often, inexperienced improvisors react to chord symbols after the fact. In other words, their solos sound like this:

A chord is sounded, the soloist plays a short idea following the chord.
A chord is sounded, the soloist plays a short idea following the chord.
A chord is sounded, the soloist plays a short idea following the chord.

The solo continues in this fashion. The result is a fragmented solo without interesting linear motion.

A good improvised solo should lead forward, either across the bar line or into the next chord, and resolve to an effective target note. Generally, primary chord tones such as the 3rd, 5th, 7th or 9th are good target notes. The 3rds and 7ths are of great importance in defining the quality of the chord (major 7th, dominant 7th and minor 7th). Also, the lowered 5th of a half-diminished chord is a crucial note in distinguishing that chord from a minor 7th chord!

Alterations of chords are also extremely attractive target notes. The #11 in a major chord clearly defines a Lydian sound. A raised 7th in a minor chord highlights a Melodic minor sound. An altered 5th or 9th in a dominant 7th chord defines the particular quality of that chord.

In a chord using a Dorian scale, the target note could literally be any note in the scale, since they are all chord tones of a minor 13th chord! The same principle applies to a Lydian, b7 scale used with a dominant 7th. The same principle applies to a Lydian scale used with a major 7th, except the root is not a good choice. The 7th is a more important note in the chord.

In the following pages, you will find two versions of several tunes: 1) the chord progression, with appropriate five-note scales that fit the sounds, and 2) the chord progression with a composed solo using all of those five-note scales and creating motives from them. In the solos, the numbers of the scale tones are shown beneath the notes.

By intention, space is minimal in the solos. This is so that as much motion as possible may be shown. Also, no chromatic embellishment is used so that the scales are clear. These solos demonstrate melodic use of the motives to create longer phrases.

Bella by Barlight
Scales

Dan Haer

Bella by Barlight
Solo

Dan Haerle

All You Think You Are
Scales

Dan Haer

All You Think You Are
Solo

Dan Haerle

(All You Think You Are, continued)

Ulterior Motive Blues
Scales

Dan Haer

Ulterior Motive Blues
Solo

Dan Haer

Solar Eclipse
Scales

Dan Haerle

Solar Eclipse
Solo

Dan Haerle

Fall Arrives
Scales

Dan Haer

Fall Arrives
Solo

Dan Haerle

Charlie's Party
Scales

Dan Haerl

Charlie's Party
Solo

Dan Haerl

Is This The Thing?
Scales

Dan Haerle

Is This The Thing?
Solo

Dan Haer[

Magic Motives
Part 5
Exercises for Playalongs

The Jamey Aebersold playalongs include many CDs that are excellent for practicing minor, major and diminished motives. The exercises in this part of the book refer to tracks that originally came from the following Aebersold CDs, which are a must for your collection of practice resources:

Volume 3 – The II-V7-I Progression

Volume 16 – Turnarounds, Cycles & II/V7s

Volume 21 – Gettin' It Together

Volume 84 – Dominant Seventh Workout

Each exercise in this part will refer to a specific track on the included CD that moves through all keys. This doesn't limit you to only that track. Be creative and experiment with other tracks from the CDs listed above.

Each exercise is notated in the first concert key of the playalong track. Using the numbers below the notes, transpose the exercise to the other 11 keys.

You may develop your own routine for the tracks on which you want to work. The tempo and/or the style may be a factor. Remember, some exercises may need to be practiced very slowly with a metronome before attempting to play them with a track! Be patient during this process. Slow, careful practice will pay off!

Five-Note Minor Scales

Five-Note Major Scales

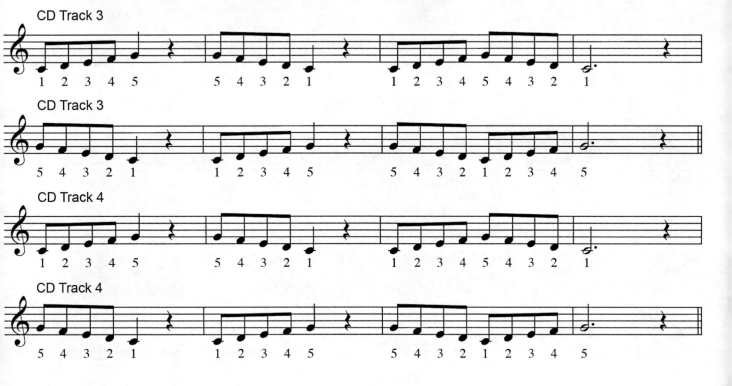

Five-Note Diminished Scales

Note: You can also play five-note minor or major scales with this track. Build the minor scale on the 3rd of each chord and the major scale on the 7th of each chord.

II-V-I Progressions

This exercise is over an unaltered II-V-I progression in all major keys. Play the five-note minor scale on the root of the II chord and on the 5th of the V chord (the same scale). Play the five-note major scale on the 5th of the I chord. Each phrase repeats before moving to the next key.

CD Track 7

This exercise is over an altered II-V-I progression in all major keys. Play the five-note minor scale on the 5th of the II chord and on the b9th of the V chord. Play the five-note major scale on the 5th of the I chord. Each phrase repeats before moving to the next key.

CD Track 7

This exercise is over an altered II-V-I progression in all minor keys. Play the five-note minor scale on the 3rd of the II chord and on the b9th of the V chord. Play the five-note minor scale on the 5th of the I chord. Each phrase repeats before moving to the next key.

CD Track 8

This exercise is over an altered II-V-I progression in all minor keys. Play the five-note major scale on the 7th of the II chord, on the #5th of the V chord and on the 4th of the I chord. Each phrase repeats before moving to the next key.

CD Track 8

Turnarounds

In these progressions, the scales used are: the half-diminished chord, a five-note minor scale built on the 3rd; the dominant 7th chords, five-note minor scales built on the b9th; the minor 7th chords, five-note minor scales built on the 5th; and the major 7th chord, a five-note major scale built on the 5th.

Try mixing motives and adding others like these:

Additional Playalong Exercises

Five-Note Major Scale Motives

Any of the five-note major scale motives in Part 6 may be practiced with the following tracks:

Track 12 (dominant 7th, 1 bar each, through the cycle)

Track 13 (major 7th, 1 bar each, through the cycle)

Track 14 (major 7th, 1 bar each, chromatically up and down)

Five-Note Minor Scale Motives

Any of the five-note minor scale motives in Part 6 may be practiced with this track:

Track 15 (minor 7th, 2 bars each, chromatically up and down)

Optional Scale Choices

Remember that you may choose other scales than the ones indicated in the playalong progressions. For example, if a five-note minor scale built on the root of a minor chord is shown, you may instead use a five-note minor scale built on the 5th or a five-note major scale built on the 7th. If a five-note major scale built on the root of a major chord is shown, you could instead use a five-note major scale built on the 5th or the 9th or a five-note minor scale built on the 3rd. On dominant 7th chords, if a five-note major scale built on the root is shown, you could also use a five-note minor scale built on the 5th or a five-note major scale built on the 9th. Altered scales will not sound good with the accompaniment unless they are specifically called for.

Magic Motives

Part 6
Sample Motives

Five-Note Major Scale Motives

Five-Note Minor Scale Motives

Five-Note Diminished Scale Motives

My Personal Motives

Magic Motives
Part 7
Thoughts on Rhythm

1. Rhythmic Modification

The rhythmic character of a motive is just as important as its melodic shape. Though a motive could be a series of continuous 8th notes, often there will be a strong rhythmic shape.

This example shows how a simple major scale became "Joy to the World," with the addition of a rhythmic shape!

Similarly, a motive consisting of only 8th notes could be given a rhythmic character like these examples:

2. Rhythmic Repetition

Repetition is an important element in all styles of music. This example shows how a typical blues melody uses melodic and rhythmic repetition. Only one motive (with an extension) is used.

3. Rhythmic/Melodic Sequences

If there is a harmonic sequence (the same progression repeated two or more times in different keys), it presents an opportunity for a rhythmic and/or melodic sequence. The following example shows a harmonic sequence of a minor II-V7 progression in three keys. The same motives are used on the half-diminished chords and the dominant 7th chords to create a perfect sequence.

Magic Motives
Part 8
Summary of Applications

(The chord tones, on which the scales are located,
are under the first notes in each example.)

Major 7th Chords

Dominant 7th Chords

Minor 7th Chords

Half-Diminished Chords

Summary of Applications (continued)

Major 7th Chords:

Five-note major scale on 1, 2 (#11), 3 (#4, #5) and 5
Five-note minor scale on 3 (#11) and 6

Dominant 7th Chords:

Five-note major scale on 1, 2 (#11), 4 (sus4) and #5 (#5, #9)
Five-note minor scale on b2 (#5, #9), 2 (sus4) and 5 (9, 9sus4)
Five-note diminished scale on 3, 5, 7 and b9

Minor 7th Chords:

Five-note major scale on 3, 4, 5 (#7) and 7
Five-note minor scale on 1 and 5

Half-Diminished Chords:

Five-note major scale on 6 and 7
Five-note minor scale on 3 and 7
Five-note diminished scale on 1

Diminished 7th Chords:

Five-note diminished scale on 1, 3, 5 and 7

Magic Motives
Concert Key Chord Progressions
(All progressions are in 4/4 time.)

MINOR – 4 bars each
Chromatically up (2 times)

Track 1

1st time – bossa
2nd time – swing

MINOR – 4 bars each
Through the cycle (2 times)

Track 2

Both times – swing

43

Track 3

MAJOR – 4 bars each
Chromatically up (2 times)

1st time – bossa
2nd time – swing

Track 4

MAJOR – 4 bars each
Chromatically down (2 times)

1st time – bossa
2nd time – swing

II-V7-I Progressions in Major
4-bar phrases repeated

Track 7

Bossa nova

(Track 7, continued)

Fine, 2nd time

II-V7-I Progressions in Minor
4-bar phrases repeated

Track 8

Swing

(Track 8, continued)

Fine, 2nd time

Turnaround Progressions
4-bar phrases repeated

Track 9

Swing

(Track 9, continued)

Fine, 2nd time

Altered V7-I in Minor, V7-I in Major
8-bar phrases repeated

Track 10

Bossa nova

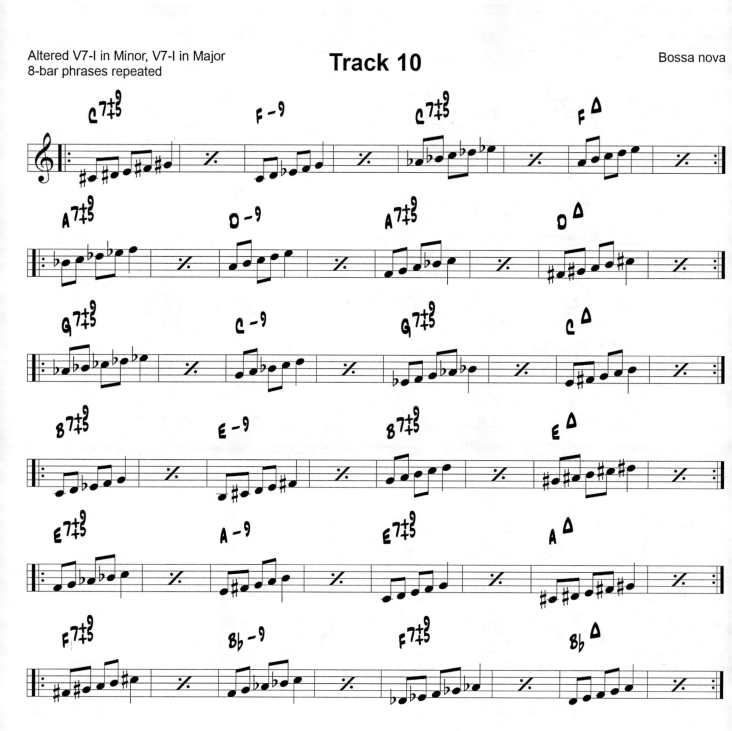

(Track 10, continued)

Fine, 2nd time

DOMINANT 7th – 4 bars each
Chromatically up, then down

Track 11

Bossa nova

54

Track 12

DOMINANT 7th – 1 bar each
Through the cycle (7 times)

Track 13

MAJOR – 1 bar each
Through the cycle (10 times)

MAJOR – 1 bar each
Chromatically up, then down (5 times)

Track 14

MINOR – 2 bars each
Chromatically up, then down (2 times)

Track 15

Magic Motives
Bb Instrument Chord Progressions
(All progressions are in 4/4 time.)

MINOR – 4 bars each
Chromatically up (2 times)

1st time – bossa
2nd time – swing

Track 1

MINOR – 4 bars each
Through the cycle (2 times)

Both times – swing

Track 2

MAJOR – 4 bars each
Chromatically up (2 times)

Track 3

1st time – bossa
2nd time – swing

MAJOR – 4 bars each
Chromatically down (2 times)

Track 4

1st time – bossa
2nd time – swing

HALF-DIMINISHED – 4 bars each
Through the cycle (2 times)

Track 5

Both times – bossa

DOMINANT 7th – 4 bars each
Random Root Movement (2 times)

Track 6

Both times – swing

II-V7-I Progressions in Major
4-bar phrases repeated

Track 7

Bossa nova

(Track 7, continued)

Fine, 2nd time

II-V7-I Progressions in Minor
4-bar phrases repeated

Track 8

Swing

(Track 8, continued)

Fine, 2nd time

Turnaround Progressions
4-bar phrases repeated

Track 9

Swing

Bb Instrument Chord Progressions

(Track 9, continued)

Fine, 2nd time

65

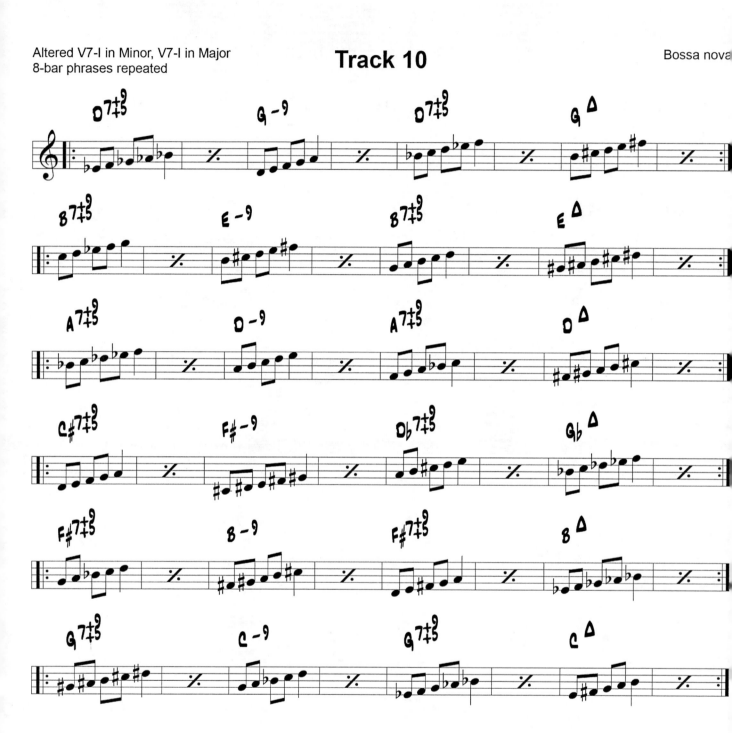

Altered V7-I in Minor, V7-I in Major
8-bar phrases repeated

Track 10

Bossa nova

(Track 10, continued)

Fine, 2nd time

67

DOMINANT 7th – 4 bars each
Chromatically up, then down

Track 11

Bossa nova

DOMINANT 7th – 1 bar each
Through the cycle (7 times)

Track 12

MAJOR – 1 bar each
Through the cycle (10 times)

Track 13

MAJOR – 1 bar each
Chromatically up then down (5 times)

Track 14

MINOR – 2 bars each
Chromatically up then down (2 times)

Track 15

Magic Motives
Eb Instrument Chord Progressions
(All progressions are in 4/4 time.)

II-V7-I Progressions in Major
4-bar phrases repeated

Track 7

Bossa nova

(Track 7, continued)

Fine, 2nd time

II-V7-I Progressions in Minor
4-bar phrases repeated

Track 8

Swing

(Track 8, continued)

Fine, 2nd time

Track 9

Turnaround Progressions
4-bar phrases repeated

(Track 9, continued)

Fine, 2nd time

Altered V7-I in Minor, V7-I in Major
8-bar phrases repeated

Track 10

Bossa nova

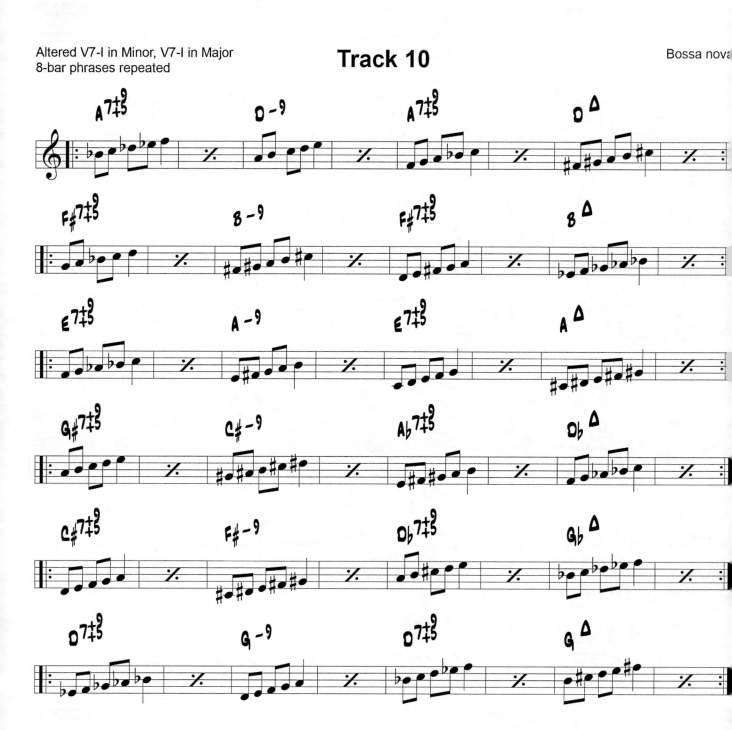

(Track 10, continued)

Fine, 2nd time

DOMINANT 7th – 4 bars each
Chromatically up, then down

Track 11

Bossa nova

DOMINANT 7th – 1 bar each
Through the cycle (7 times)

Track 12

MAJOR – 1 bar each
Through the cycle (10 times)

Track 13

MAJOR – 1 bar each
Chromatically up then down (5 times)

Track 14

MINOR – 2 bars each
Chromatically up then down (2 times)

Track 15

Magic Motives
Bass Clef Instrument Chord Progressions
(All progressions are in 4/4 time.)

MINOR – 4 bars each
Chromatically up (2 times)

Track 1

1st time – bossa
2nd time – swing

MINOR – 4 bars each
Through the cycle (2 times)

Track 2

Both times – swing

HALF-DIMINISHED – 4 bars each
Through the cycle (2 times)

Track 5

Both times – bossa

DOMINANT 7th – 4 bars each
Random Root Movement (2 times)

Track 6

Both times – swing

II-V7-I Progressions in Major
4-bar phrases repeated

Track 7

Bossa nova

(Track 7, continued)

Fine, 2nd time

II-V7-I Progressions in Minor
4-bar phrases repeated

Track 8

Swin

(Track 8, continued)

Fine, 2nd time

Turnaround Progressions
4-bar phrases repeated

Track 9

Swir

(Track 9, continued)

Fine, 2nd time

Altered V7-I in Minor, V7-I in Major
8-bar phrases repeated

Track 10

Bossa nova

(Track 10, continued)

Fine, 2nd time

DOMINANT 7th – 4 bars each
Chromatically up, then down

Track 11

Bossa nova

DOMINANT 7th – 1 bar each
Through the cycle (7 times)

Track 12

MAJOR – 1 bar each
Through the cycle (10 times)

Track 13

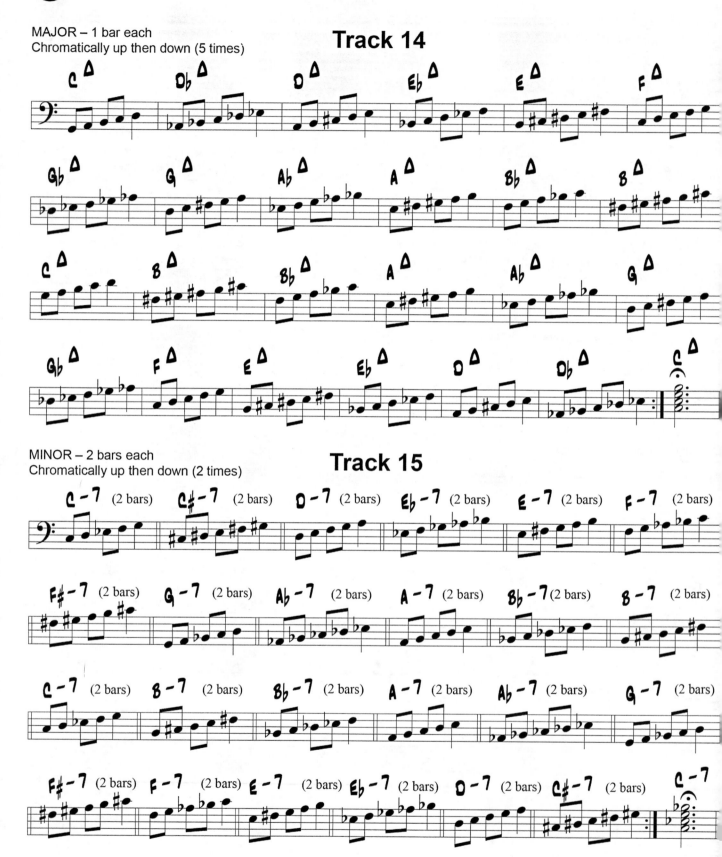